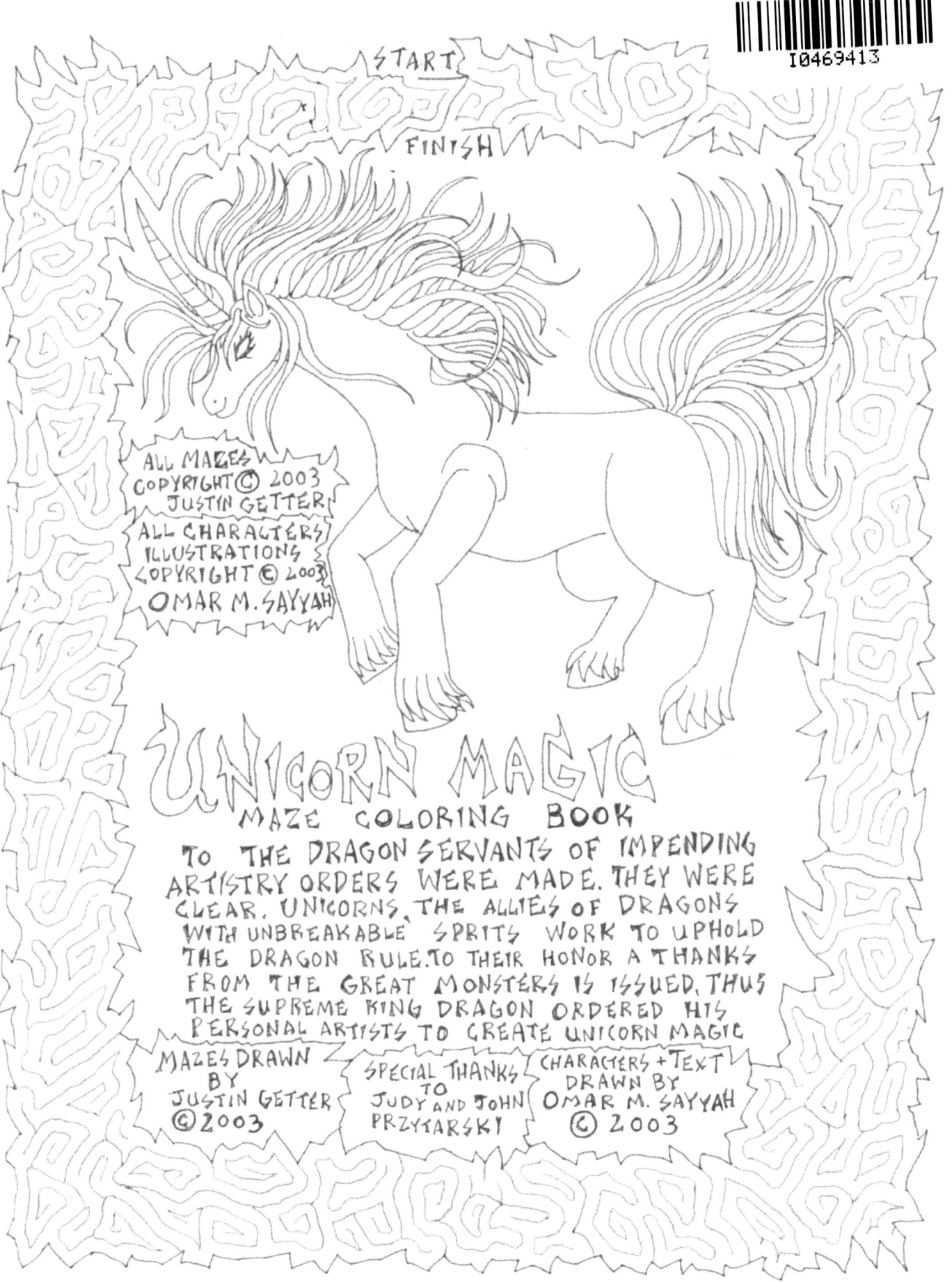

START

FINISH

UNICORN MAGIC

MAZE COLORING BOOK

TO THE DRAGON SERVANTS OF IMPENDING
ARTISTRY ORDERS WERE MADE. THEY WERE
CLEAR. UNICORNS, THE ALLIES OF DRAGONS
WITH UNBREAKABLE SPRITS WORK TO UPHOLD
THE DRAGON RULE. TO THEIR HONOR A THANKS
FROM THE GREAT MONSTERS IS ISSUED. THUS
THE SUPREME KING DRAGON ORDERED HIS
PERSONAL ARTISTS TO CREATE UNICORN MAGIC

MAZES DRAWN
BY
JUSTIN GETTER
© 2003

SPECIAL THANKS
TO
JUDY AND JOHN
PRZYTARSKI

CHARACTERS + TEXT
DRAWN BY
OMAR M. SAYYAH
© 2003

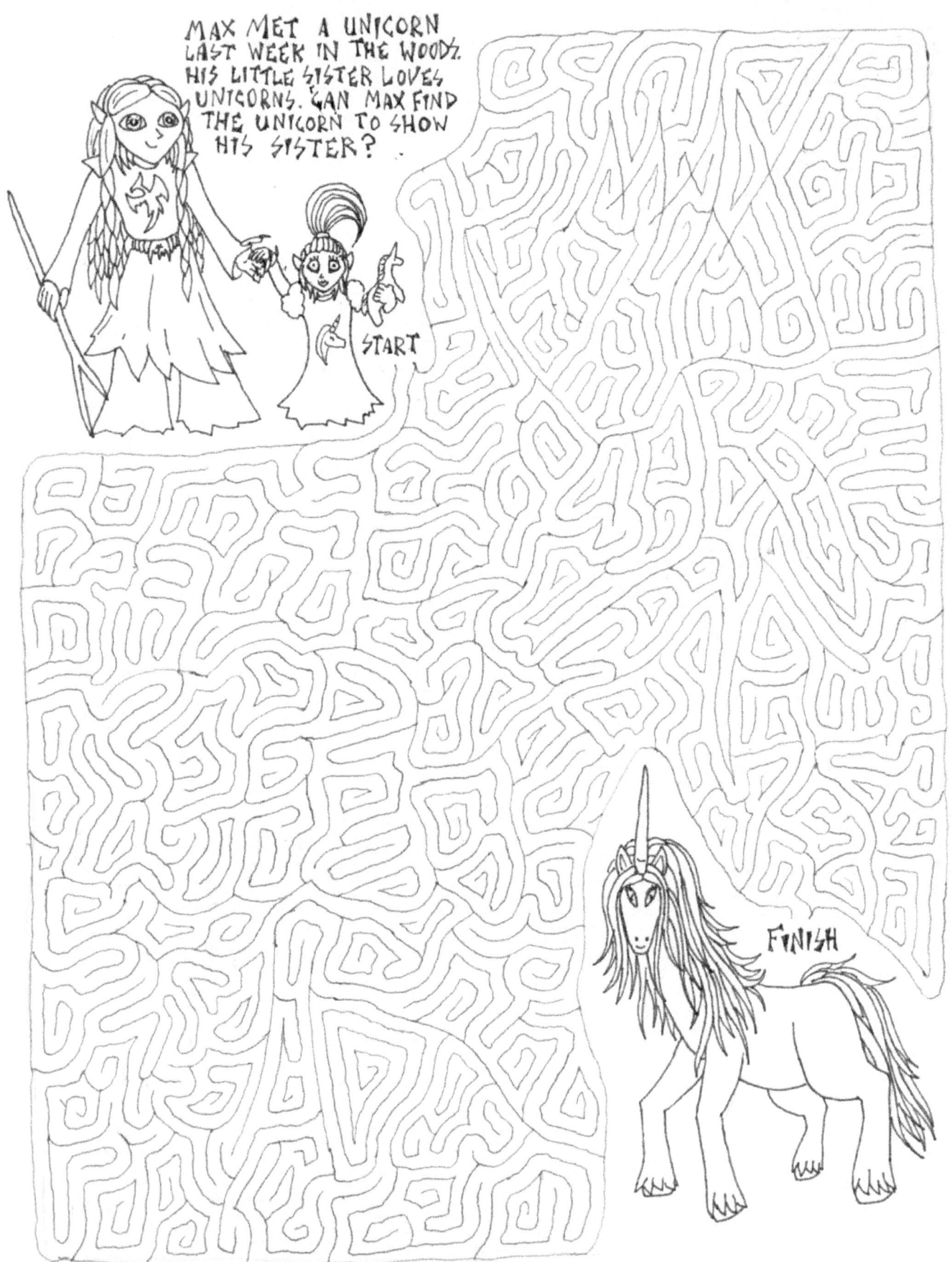

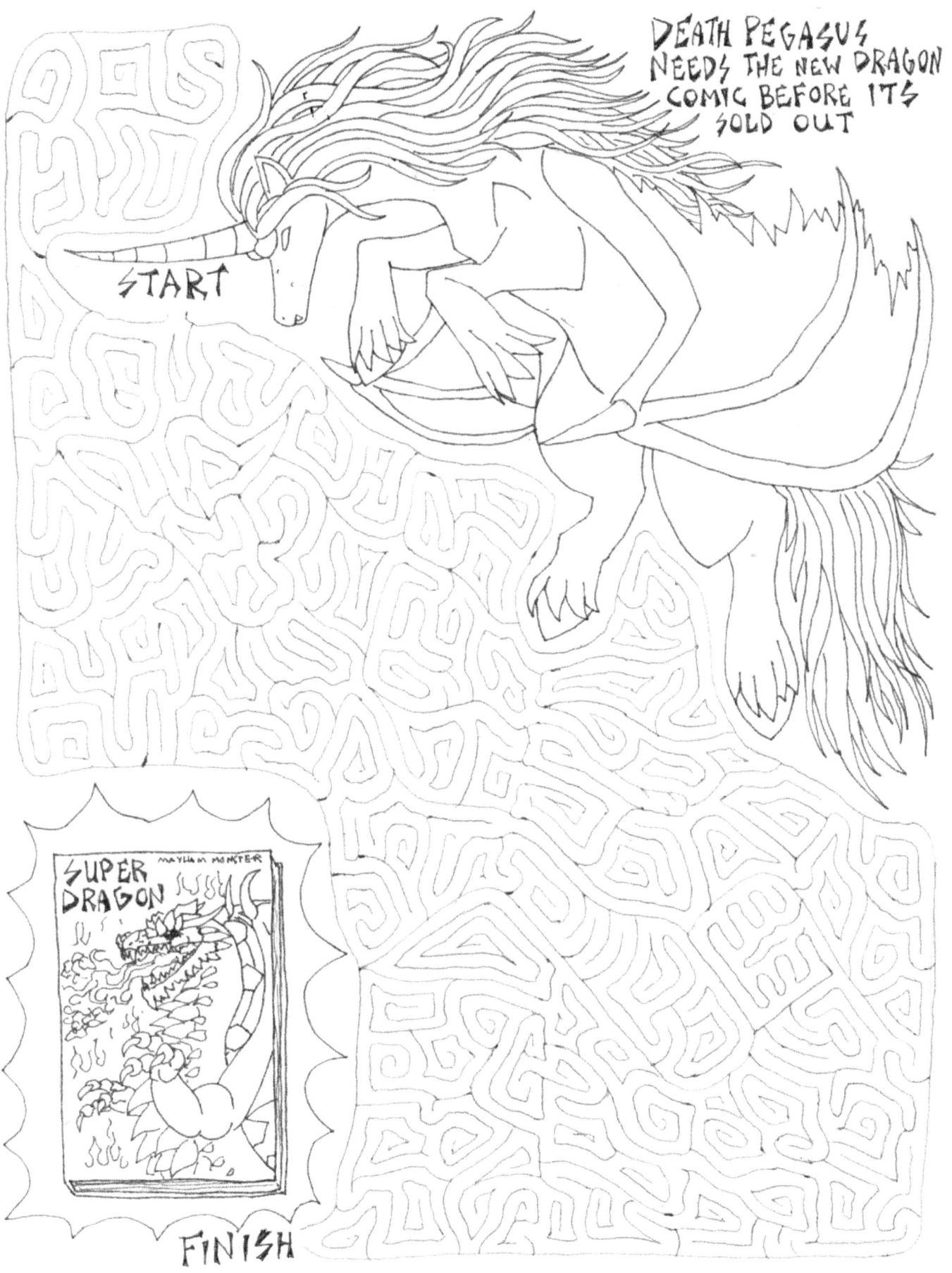

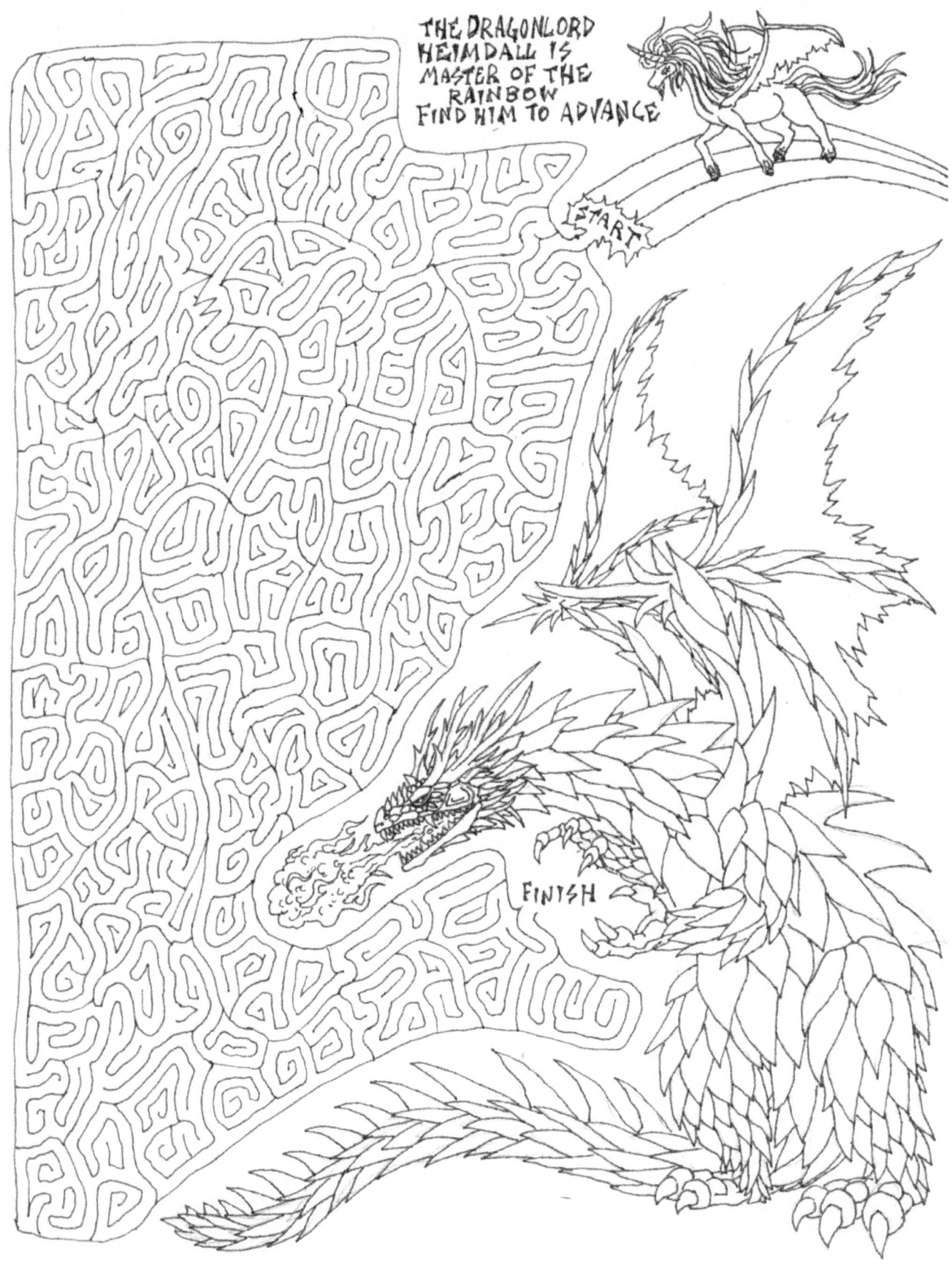

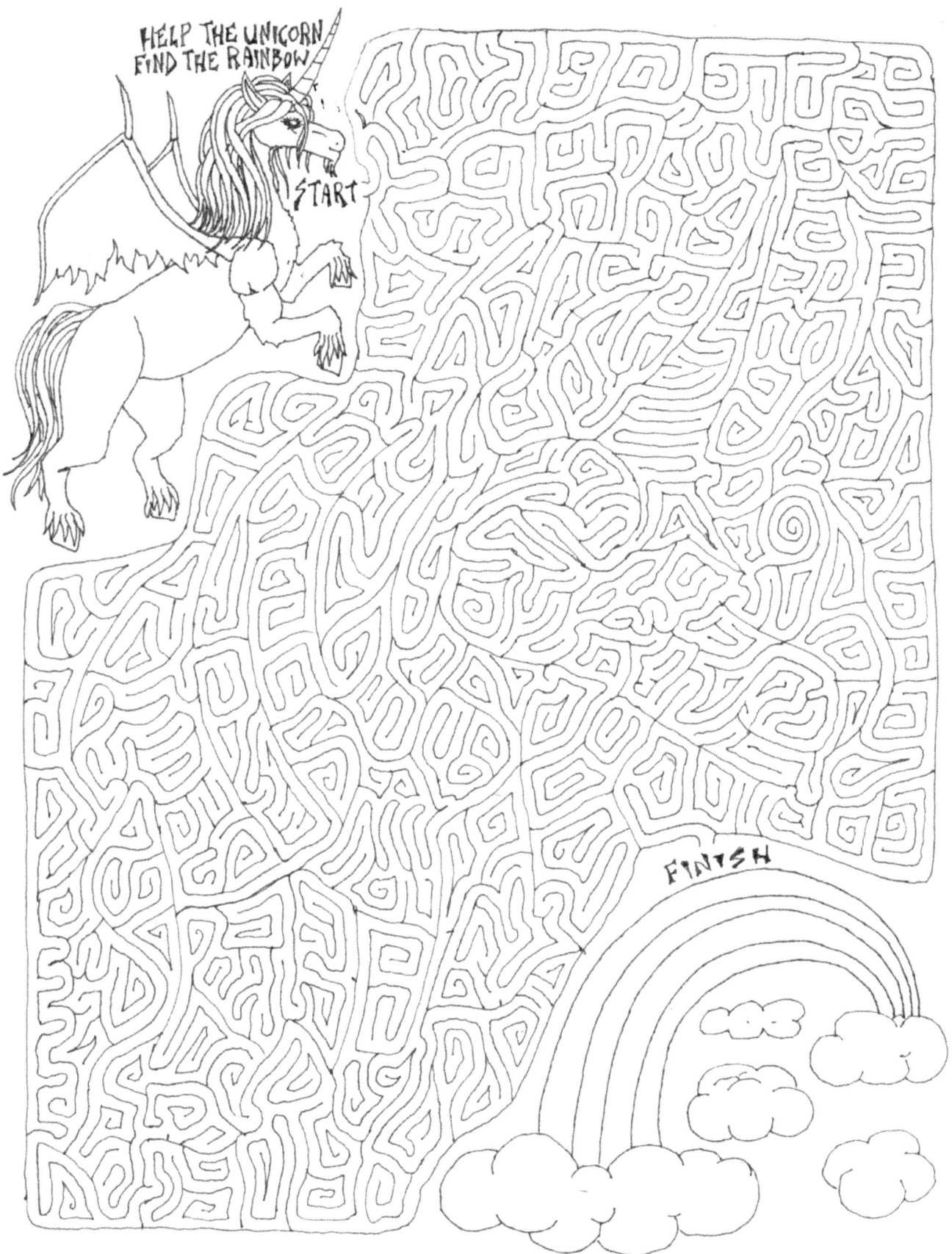

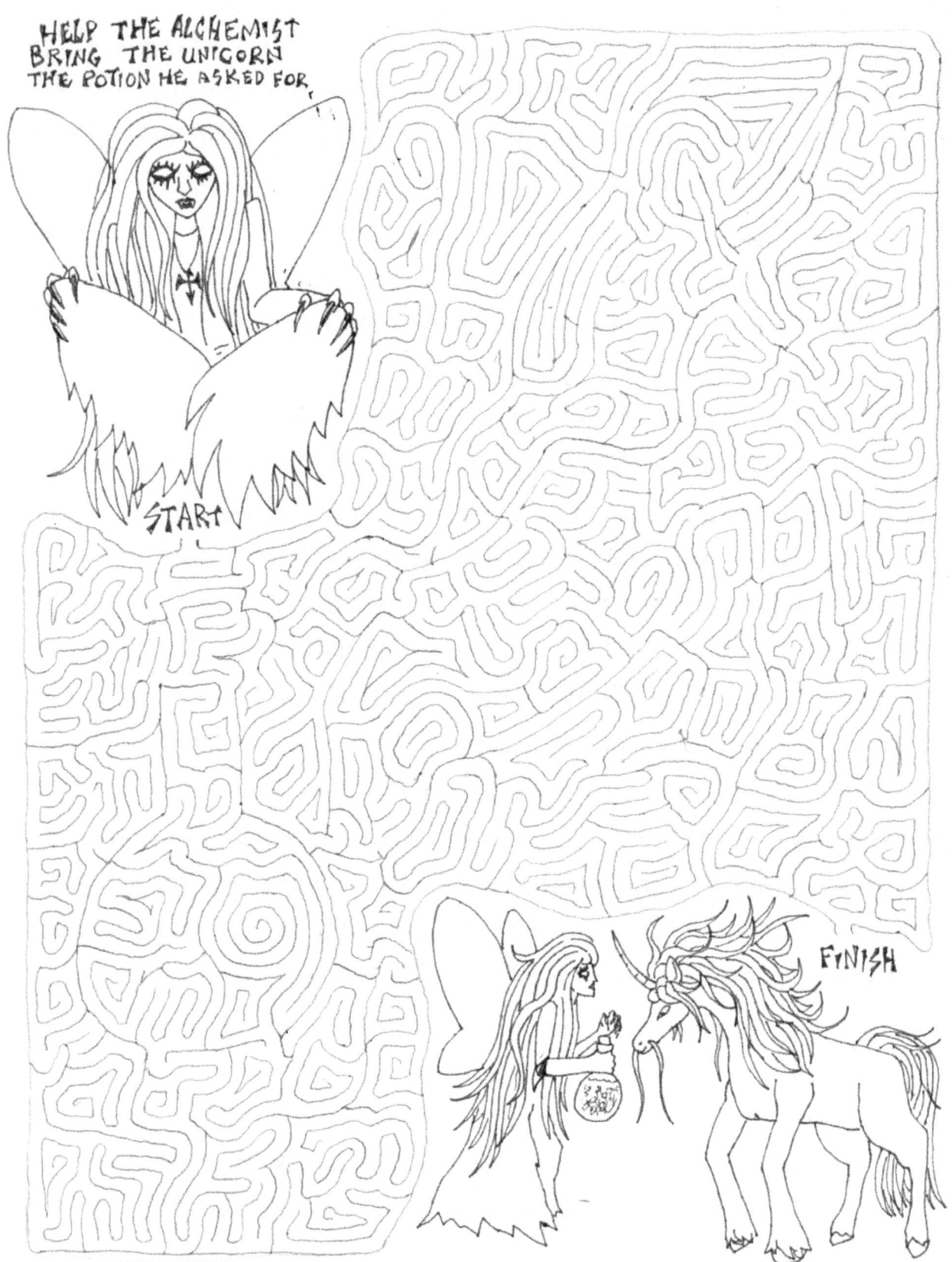

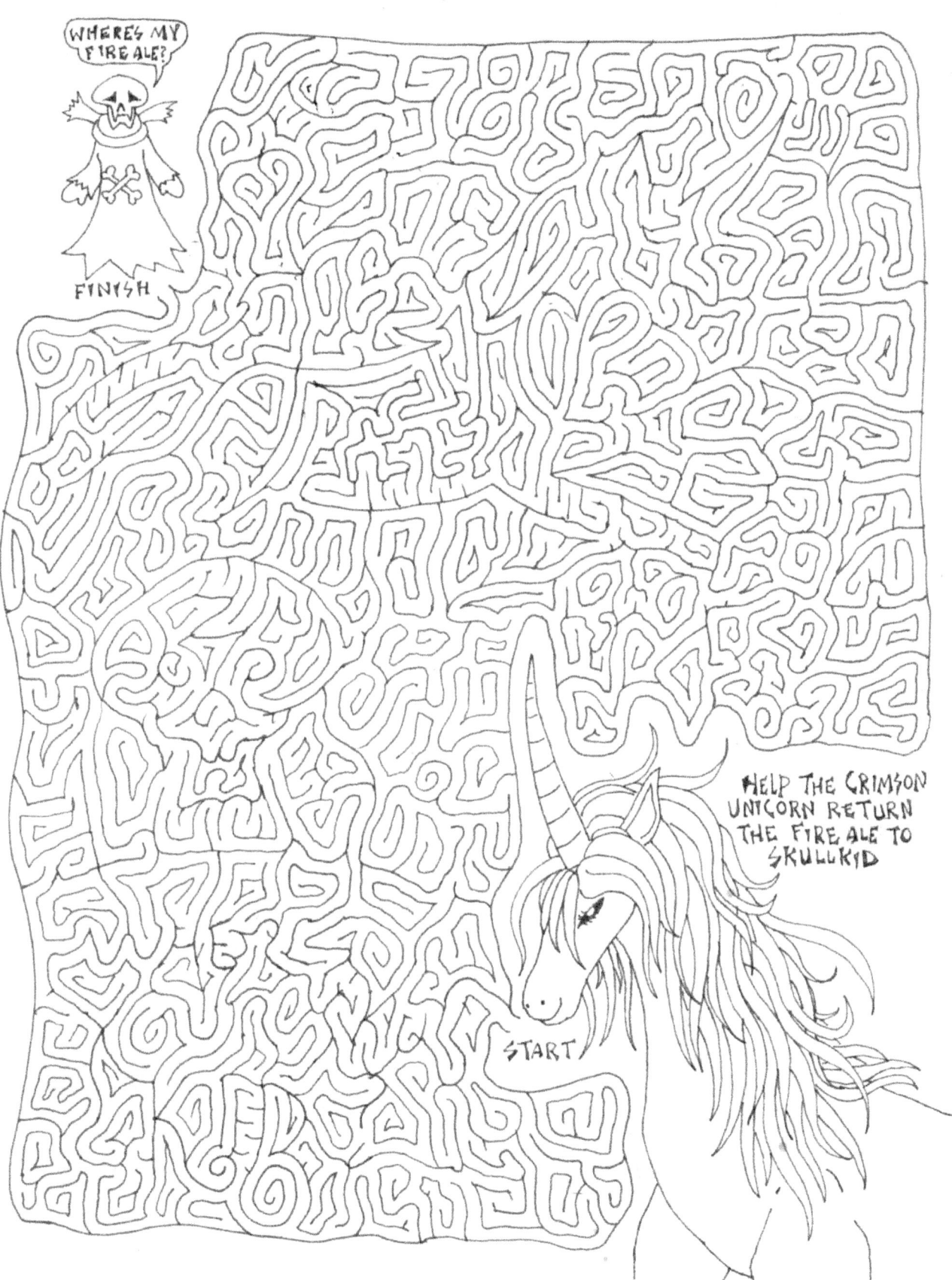

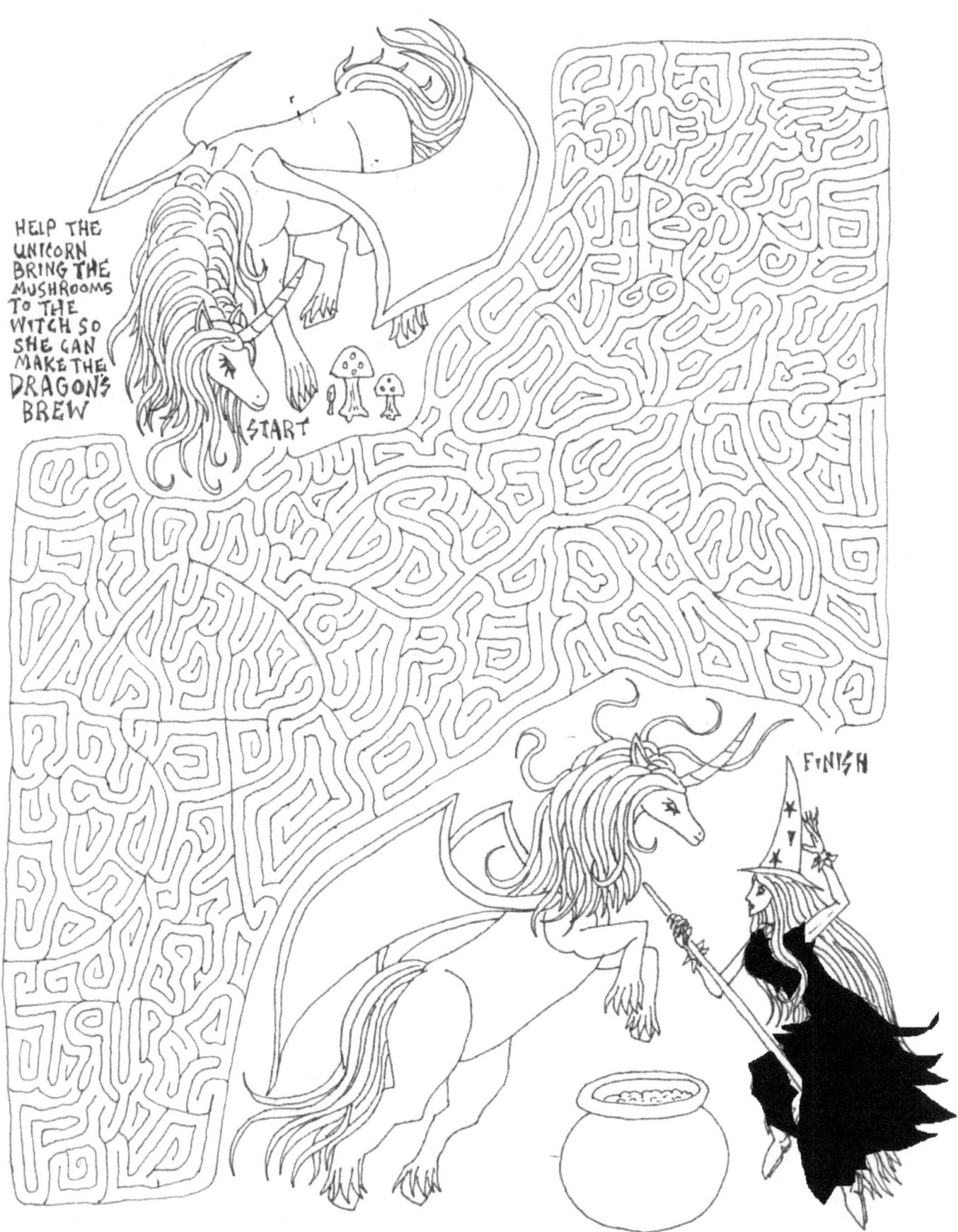

HELP THE
UNICORN
BRING THE
MUSHROOMS
TO THE
WITCH SO
SHE CAN
MAKE THE
DRAGON'S
BREW

START

FINISH

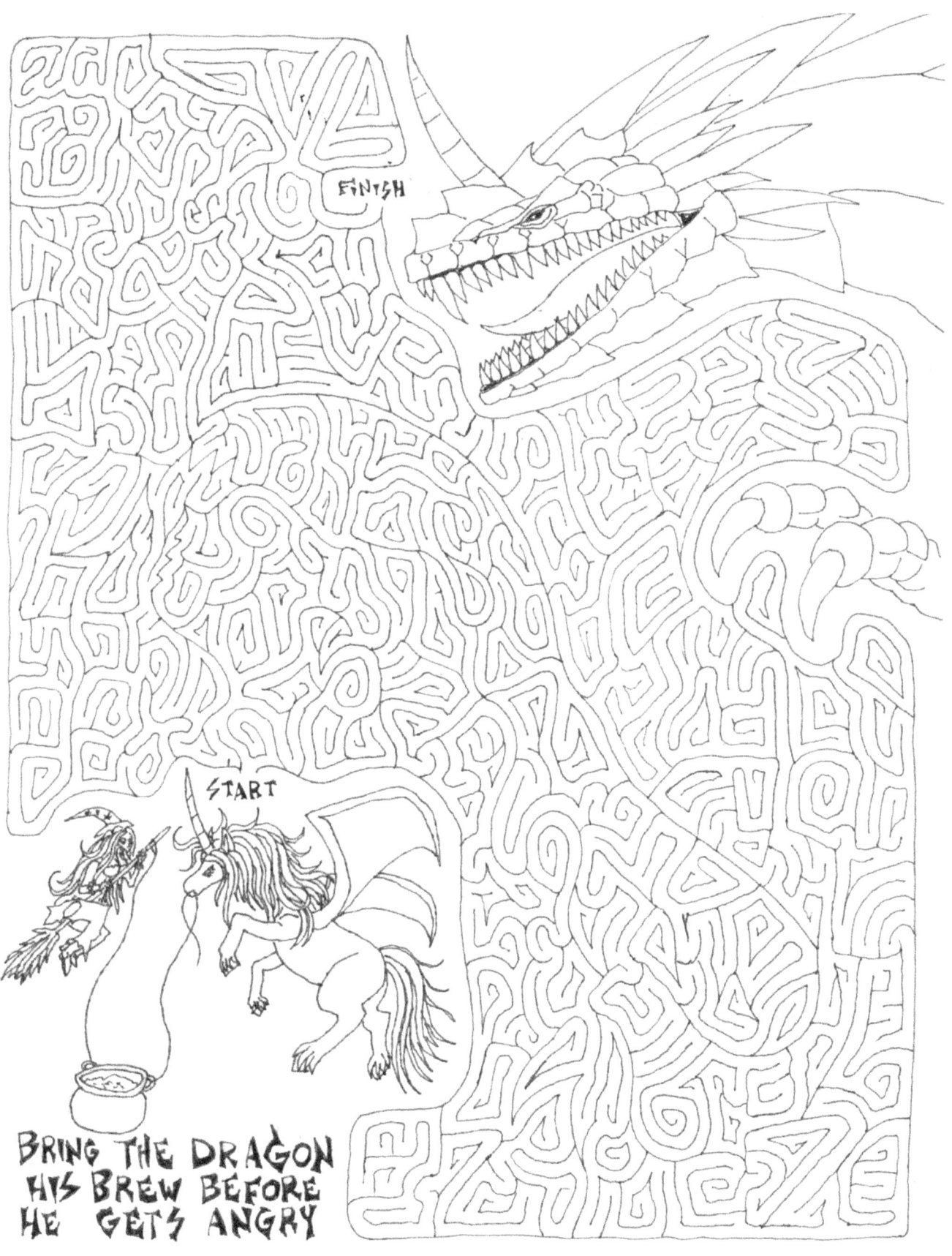

FINISH

START

BRING THE DRAGON
HIS BREW BEFORE
HE GETS ANGRY

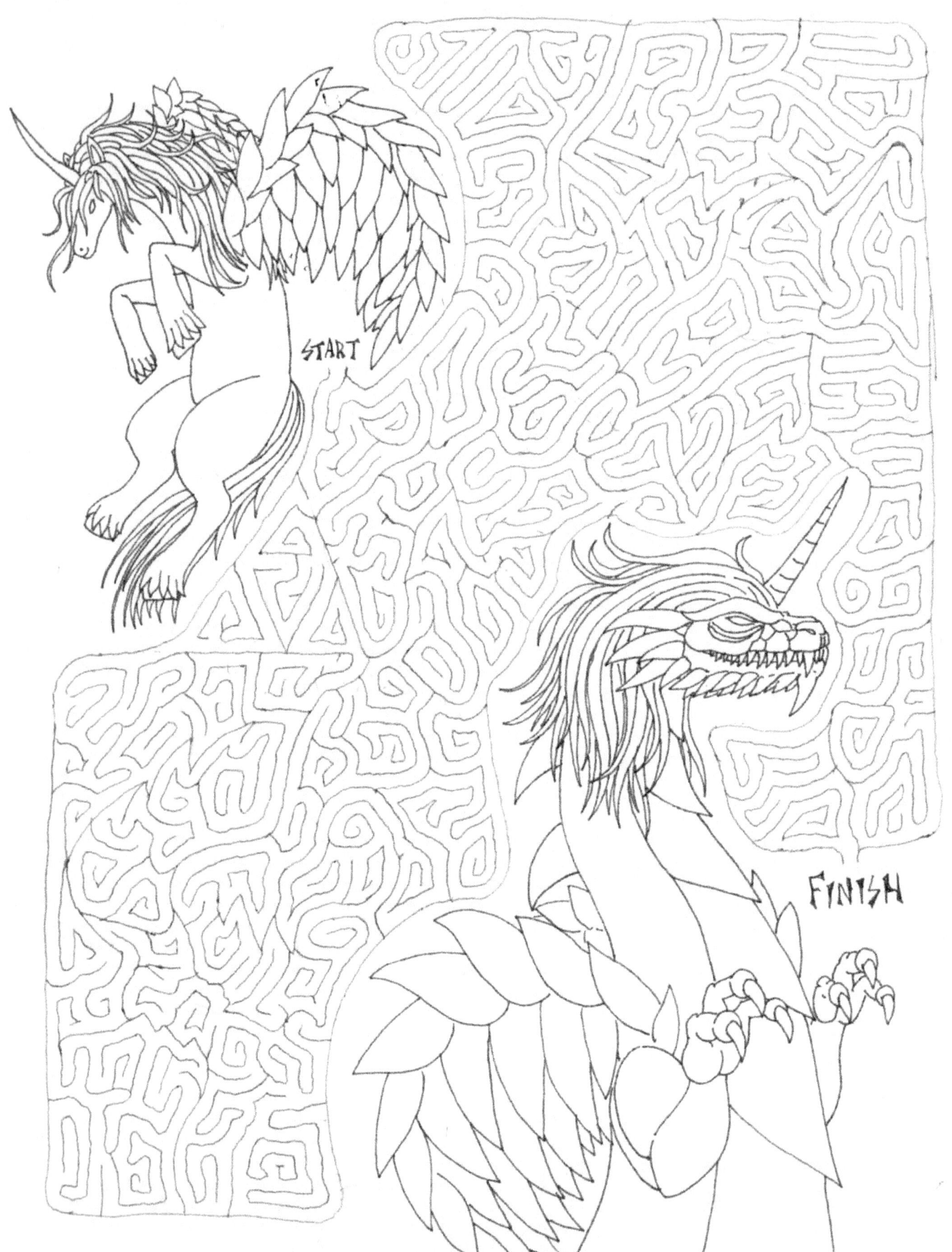

START

FYNISH

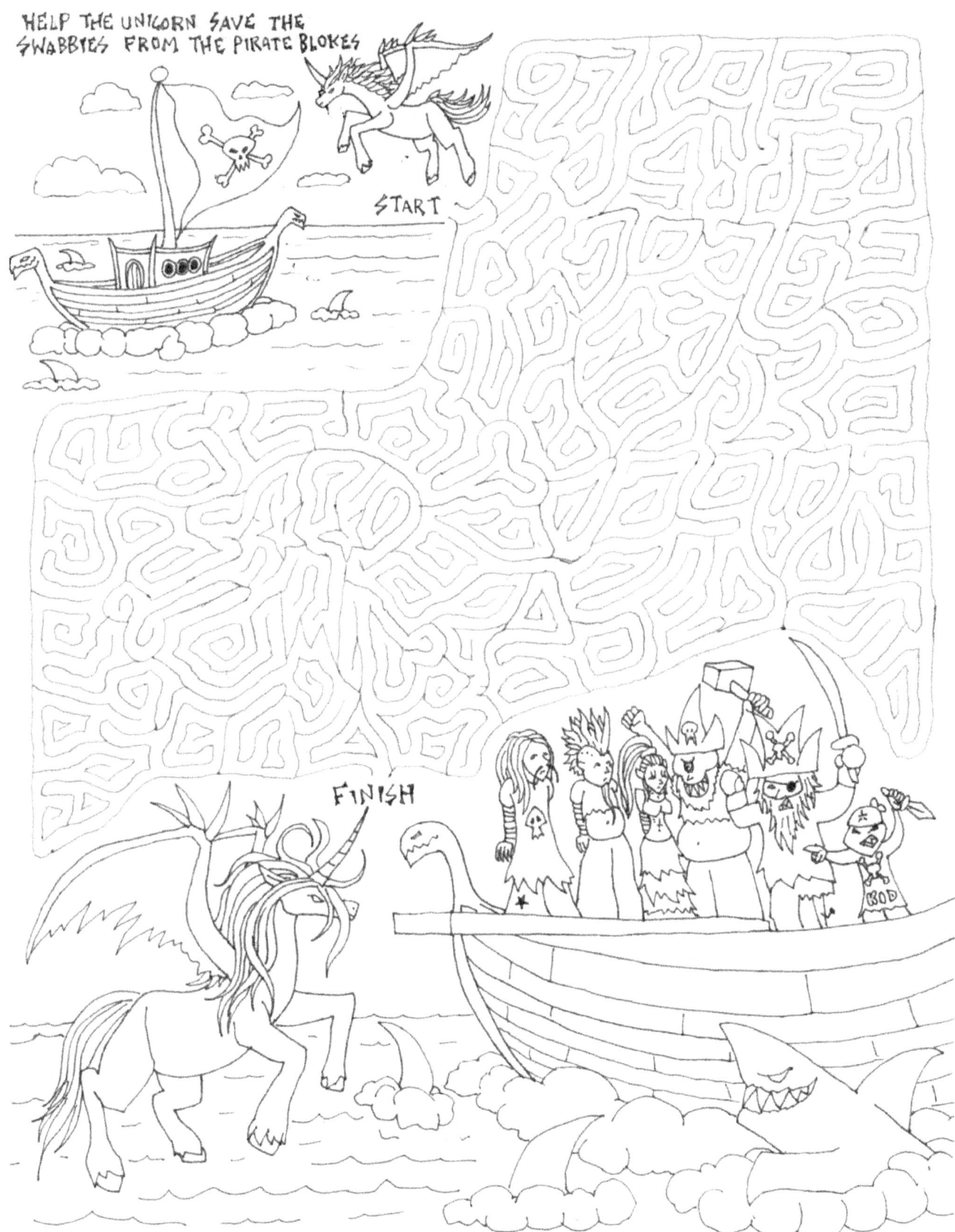

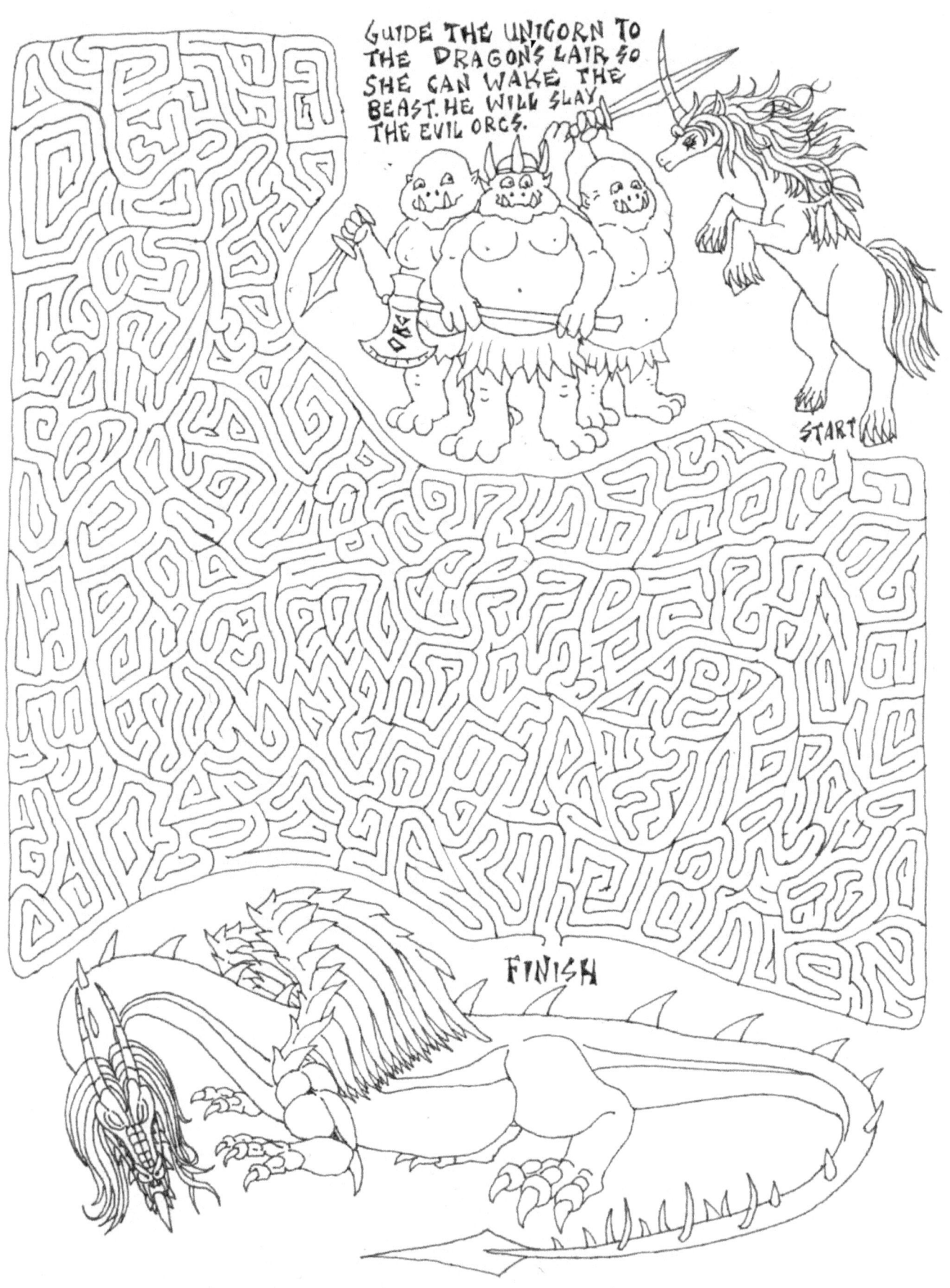

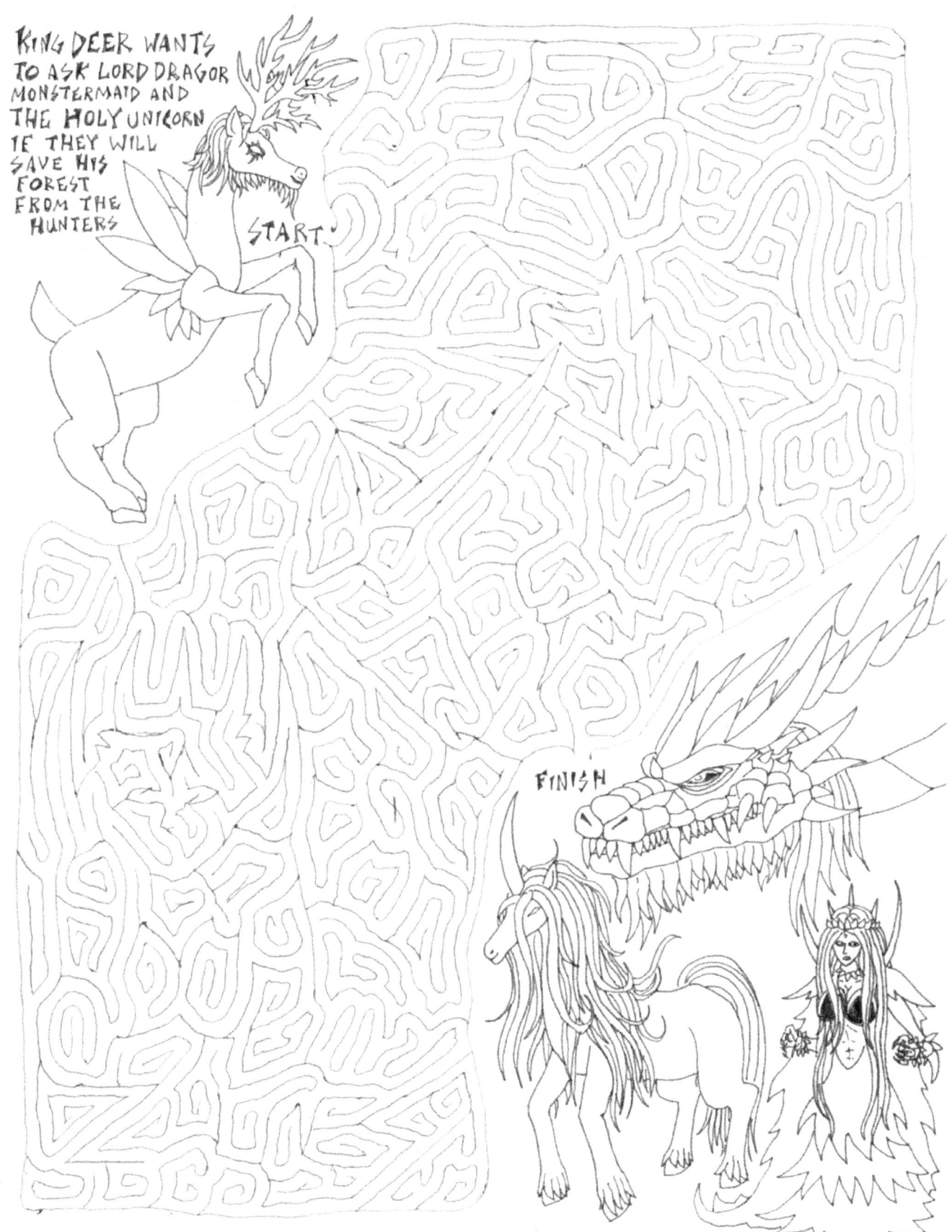

KING DEER WANTS
TO ASK LORD DRAGOR
MONSTERMAID AND
THE HOLY UNICORN
IF THEY WILL
SAVE HIS
FOREST
FROM THE
HUNTERS

START

FINISH

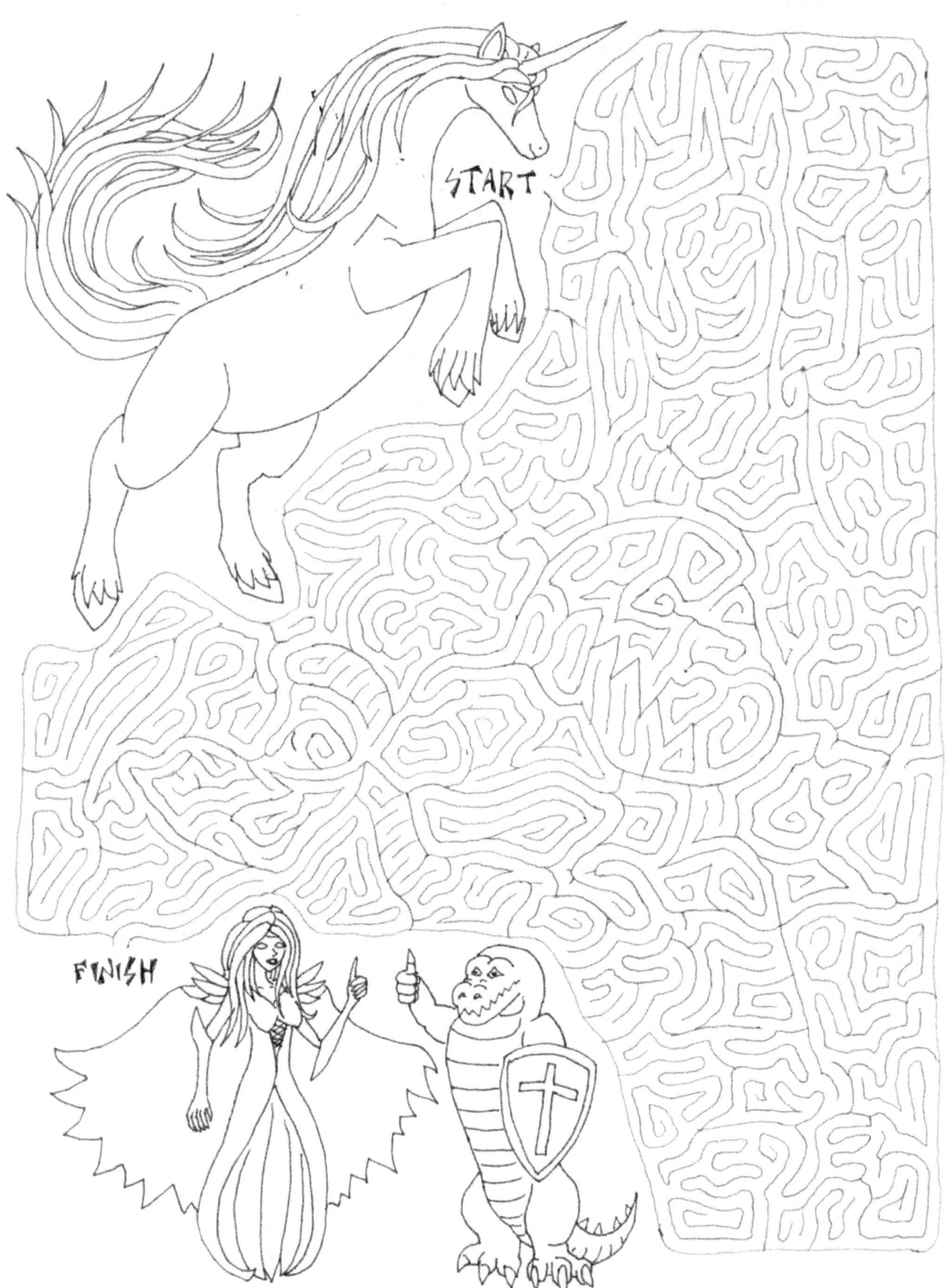

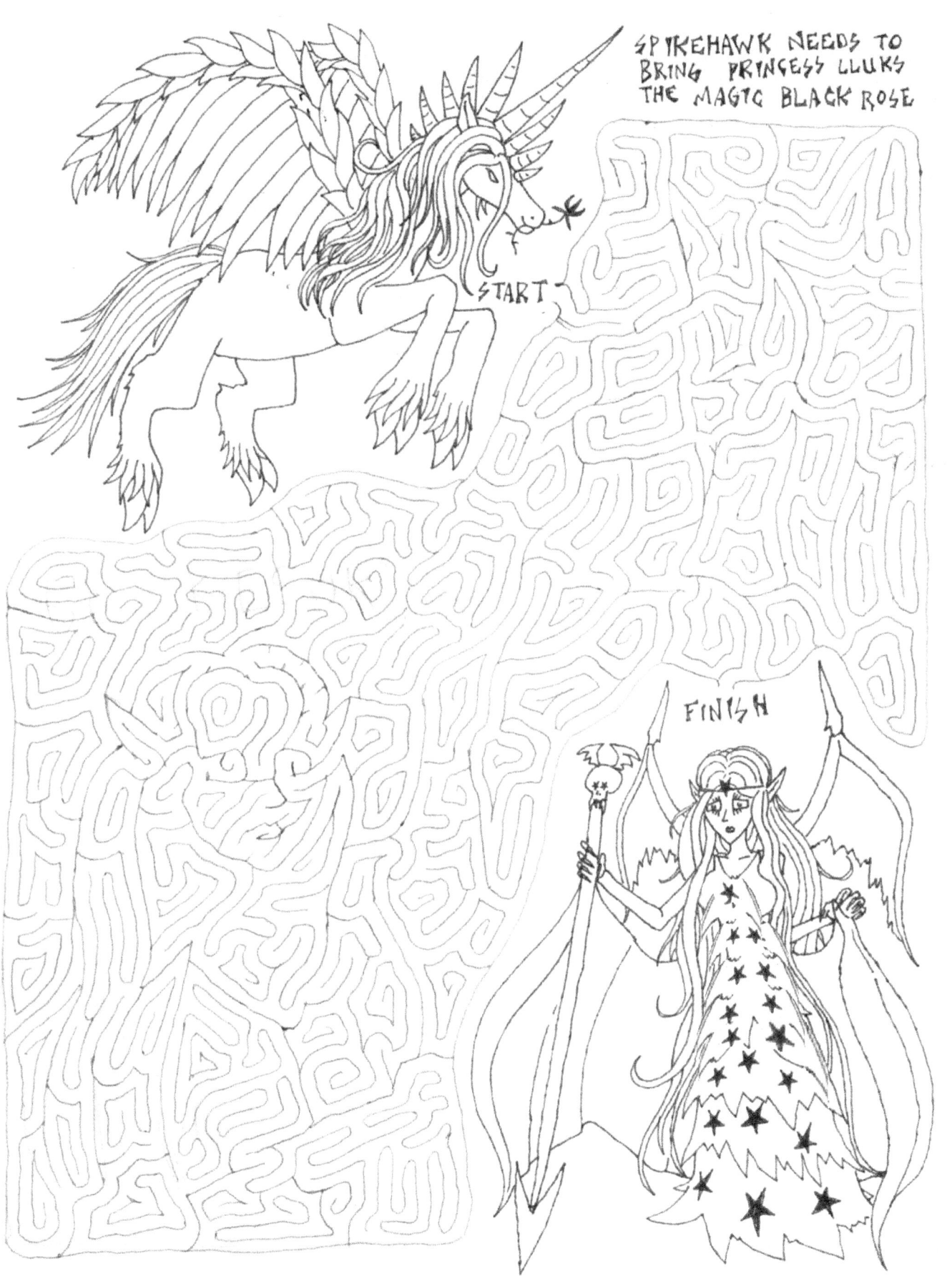

SPIKEHAWK NEEDS TO
BRING PRINCESS LLUKS
THE MAGIC BLACK ROSE

START

FINISH

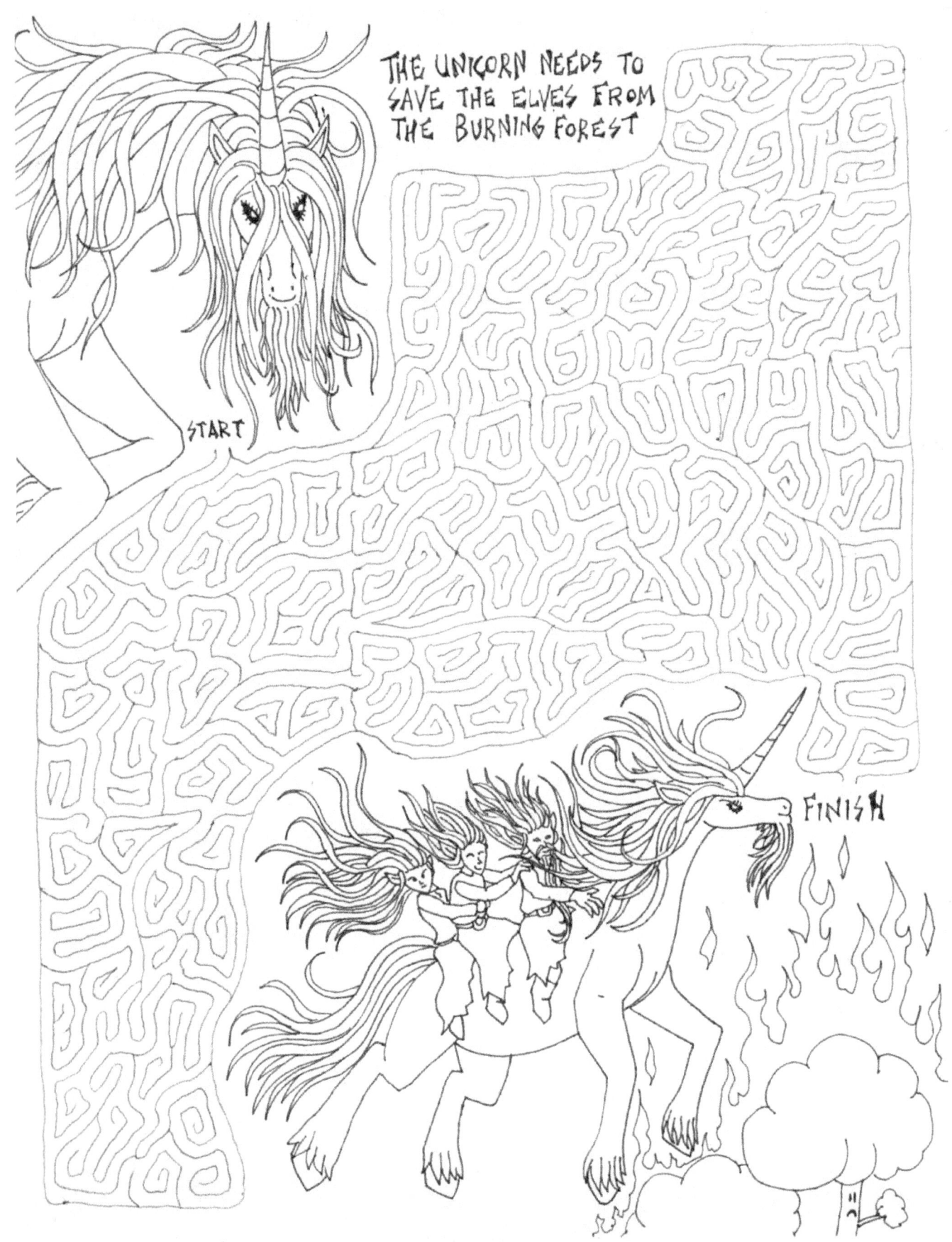

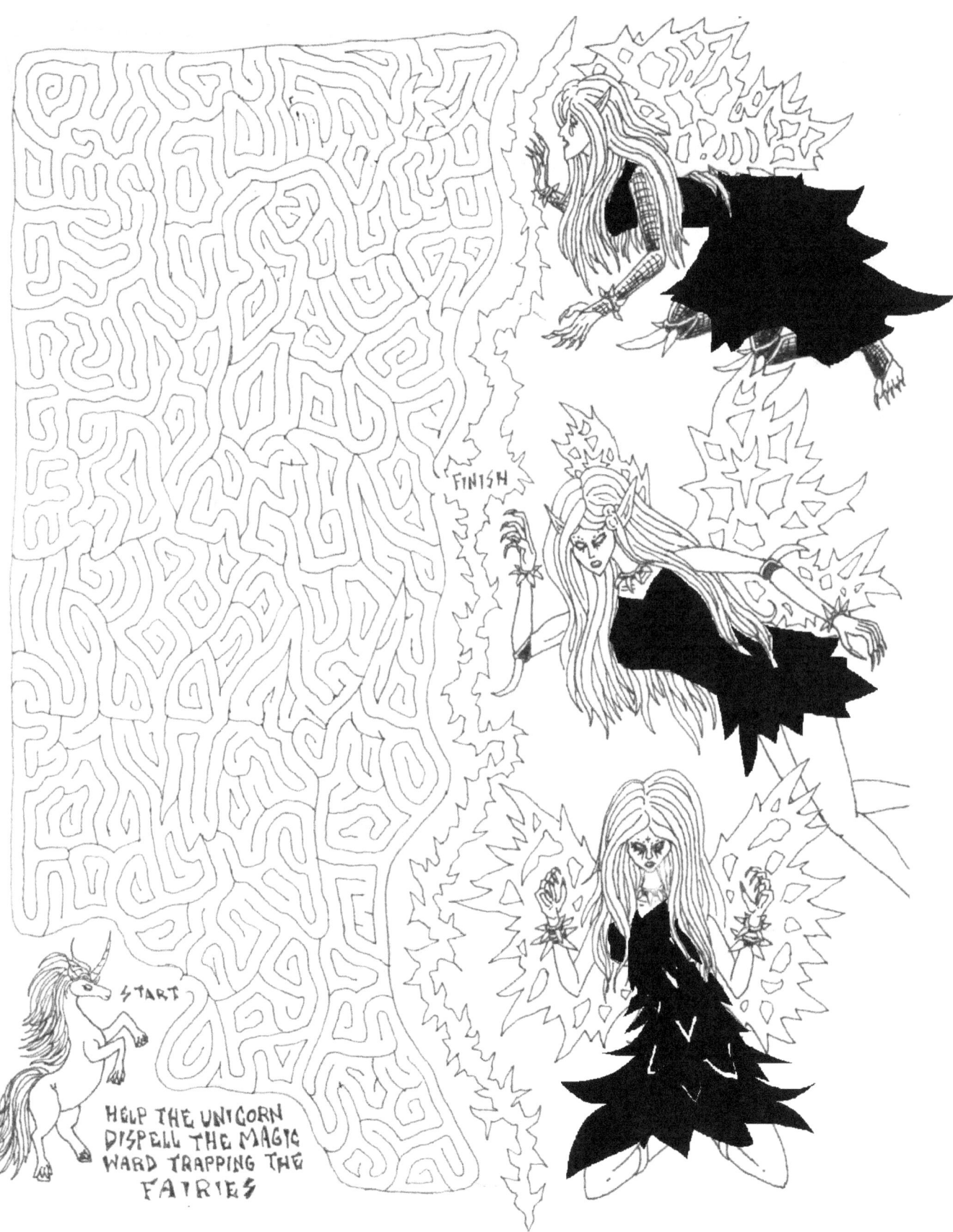

FINISH

START

HELP THE UNICORN
DISPELL THE MAGIC
WARD TRAPPING THE
FAIRIES

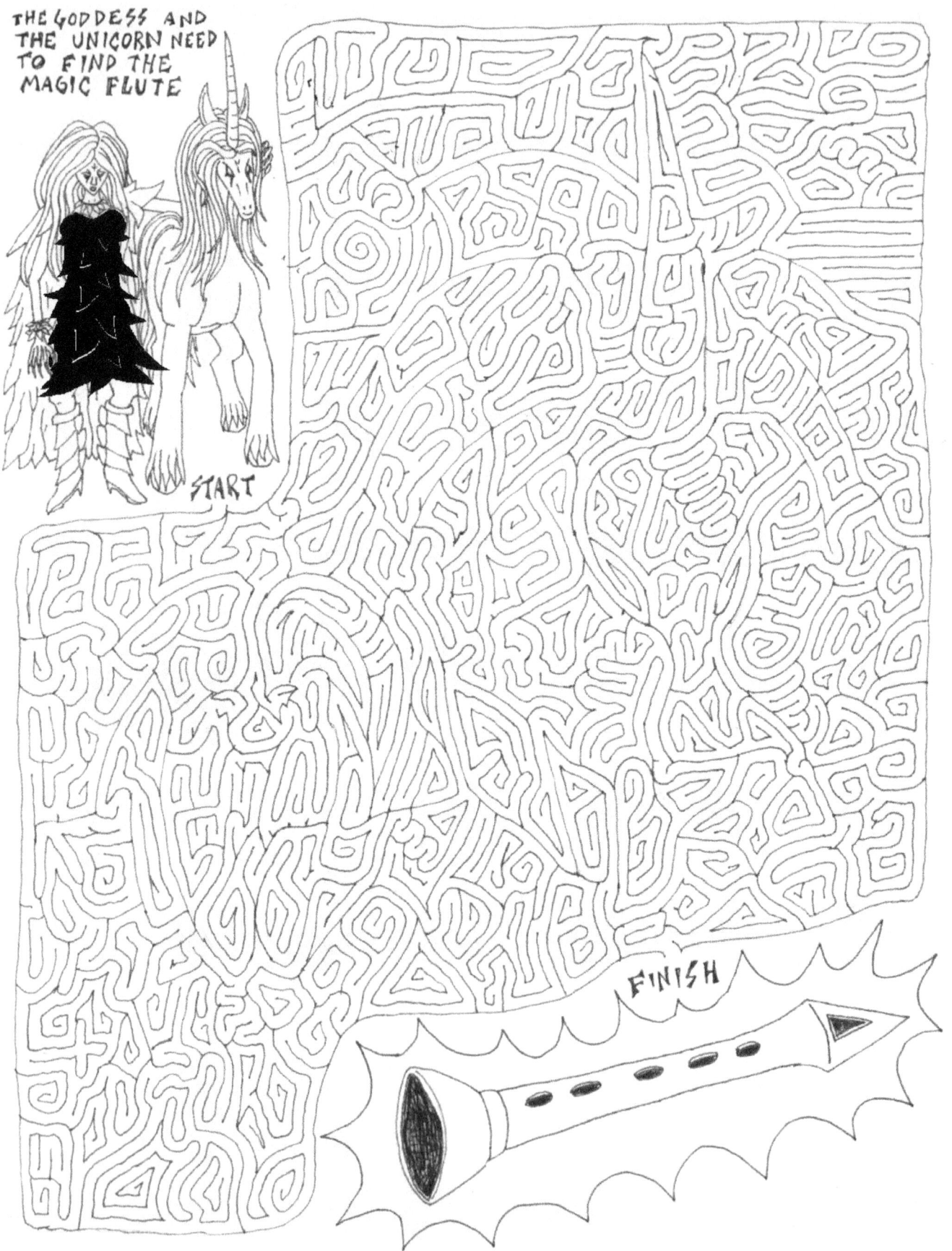

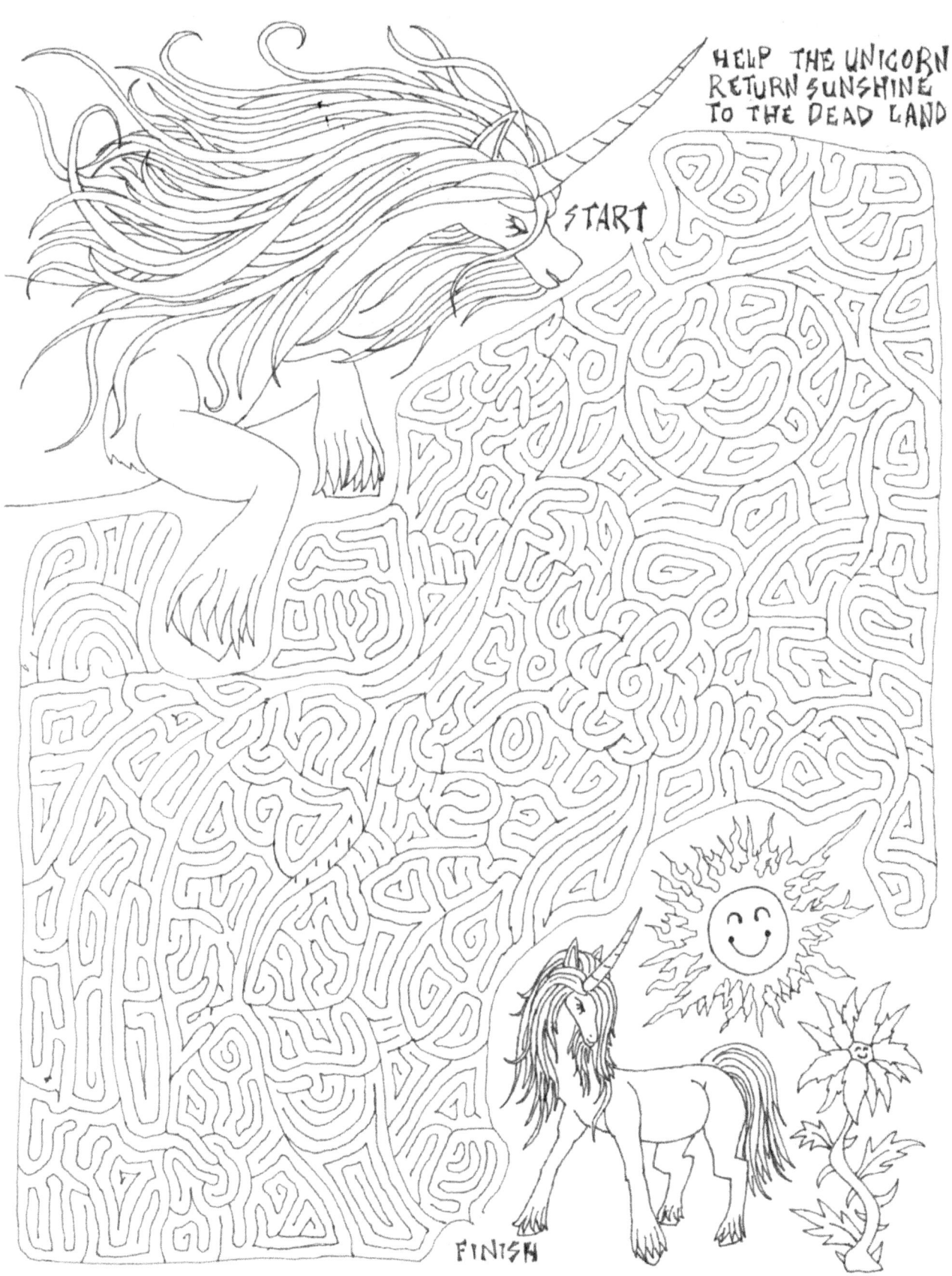

HELP THE UNICORN
RETURN SUNSHINE
TO THE DEAD LAND

START

FINISH

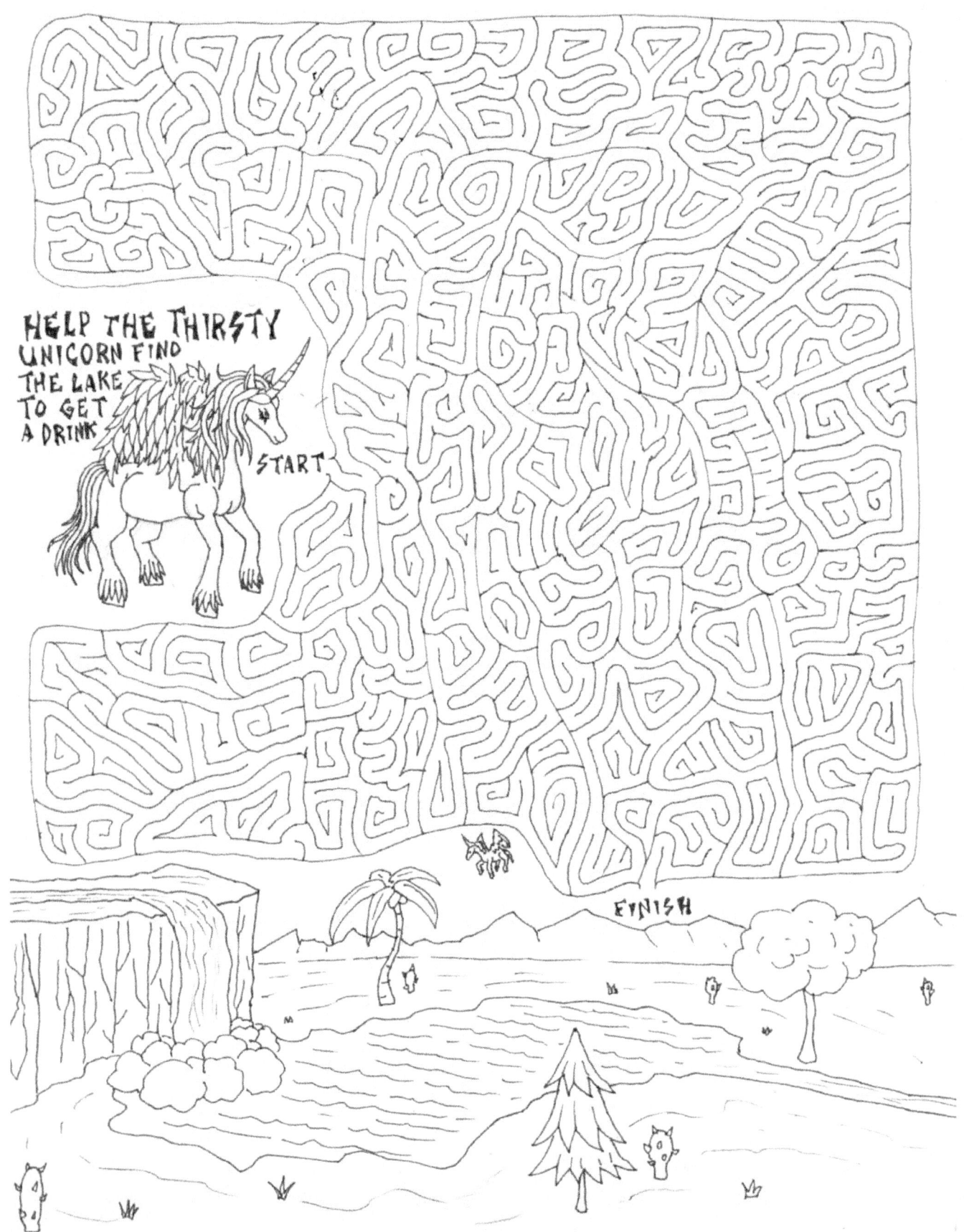

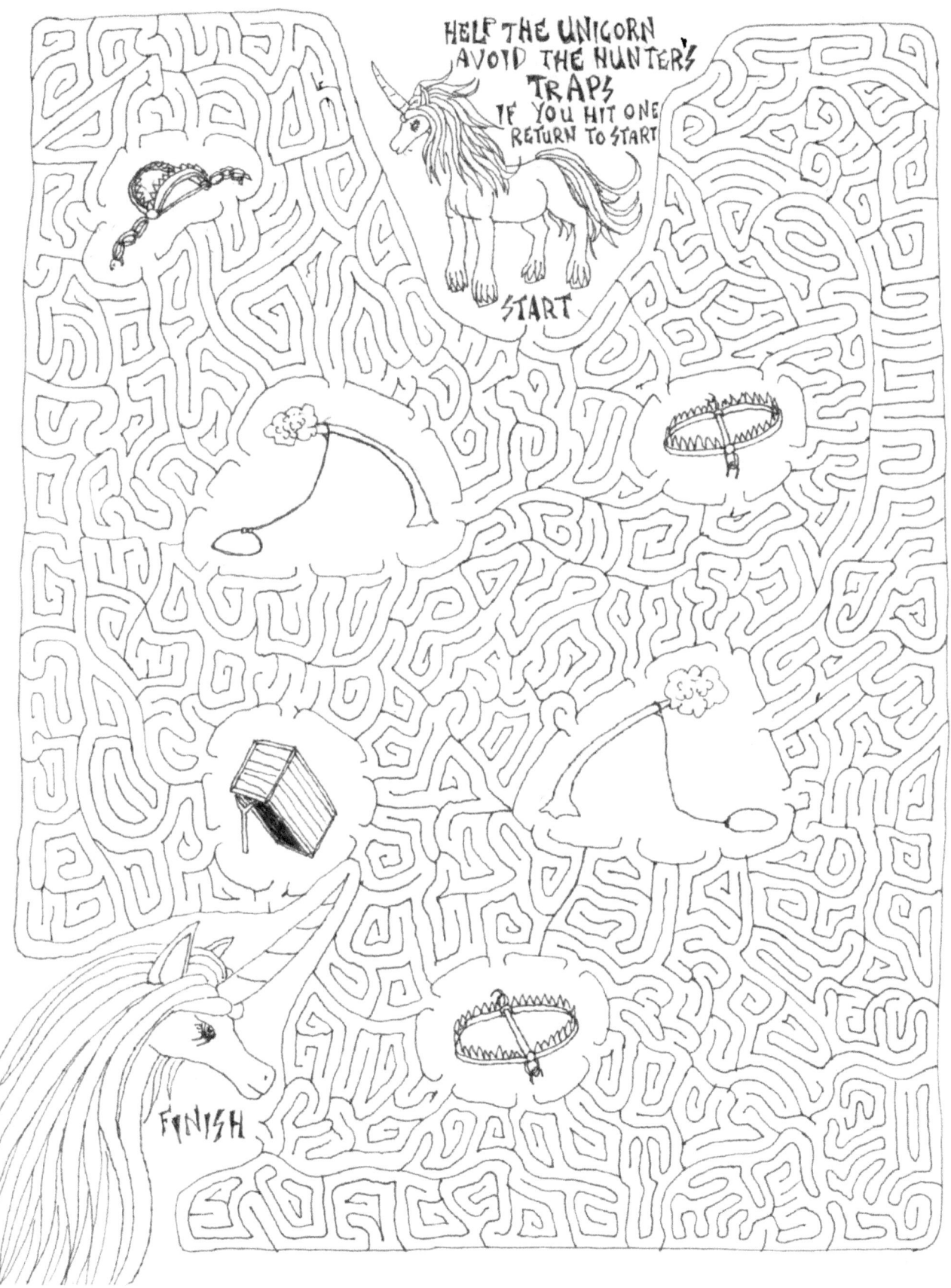

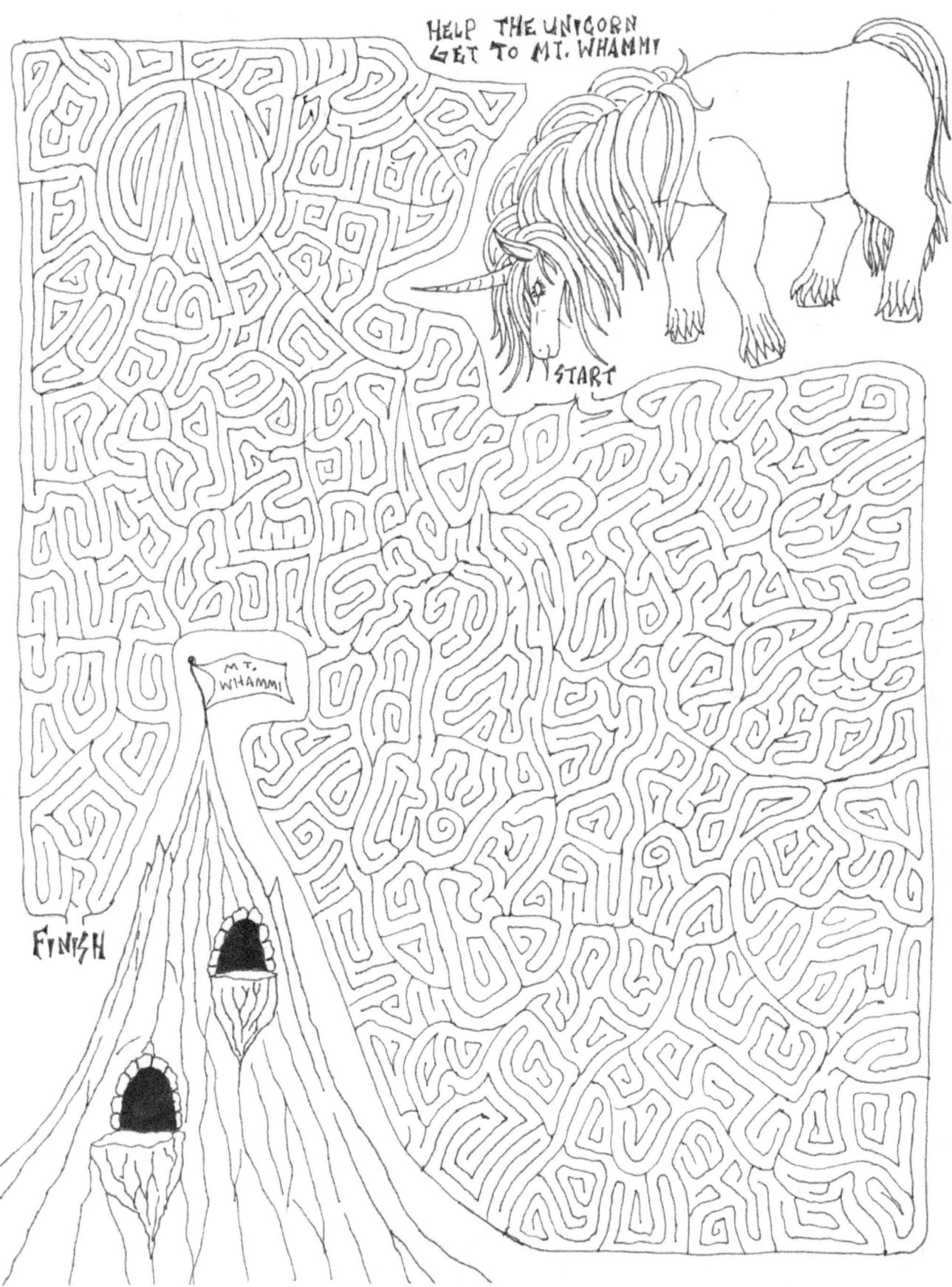

HELP THE UNICORN FIND THE LOST KID

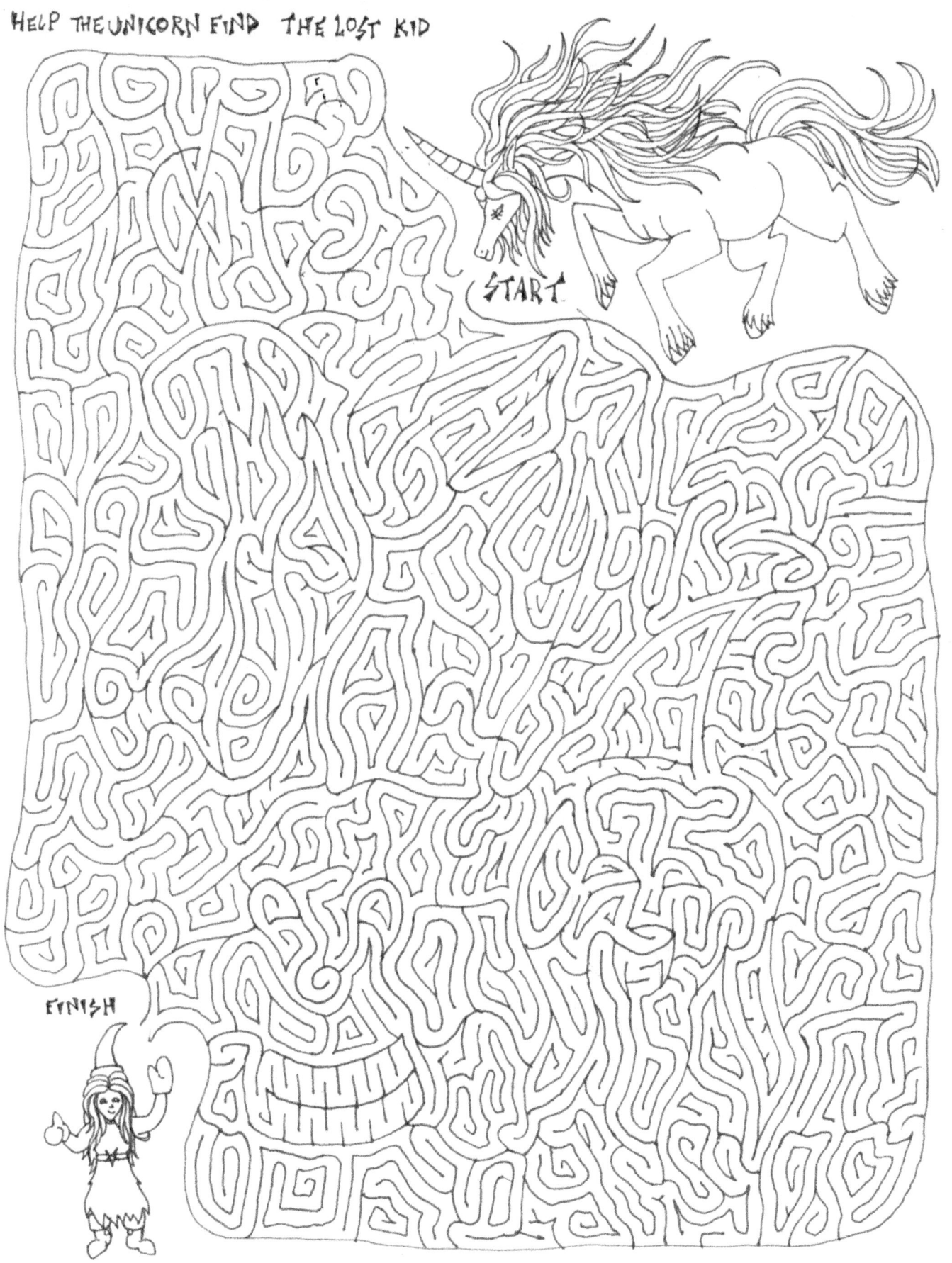

START

FINISH

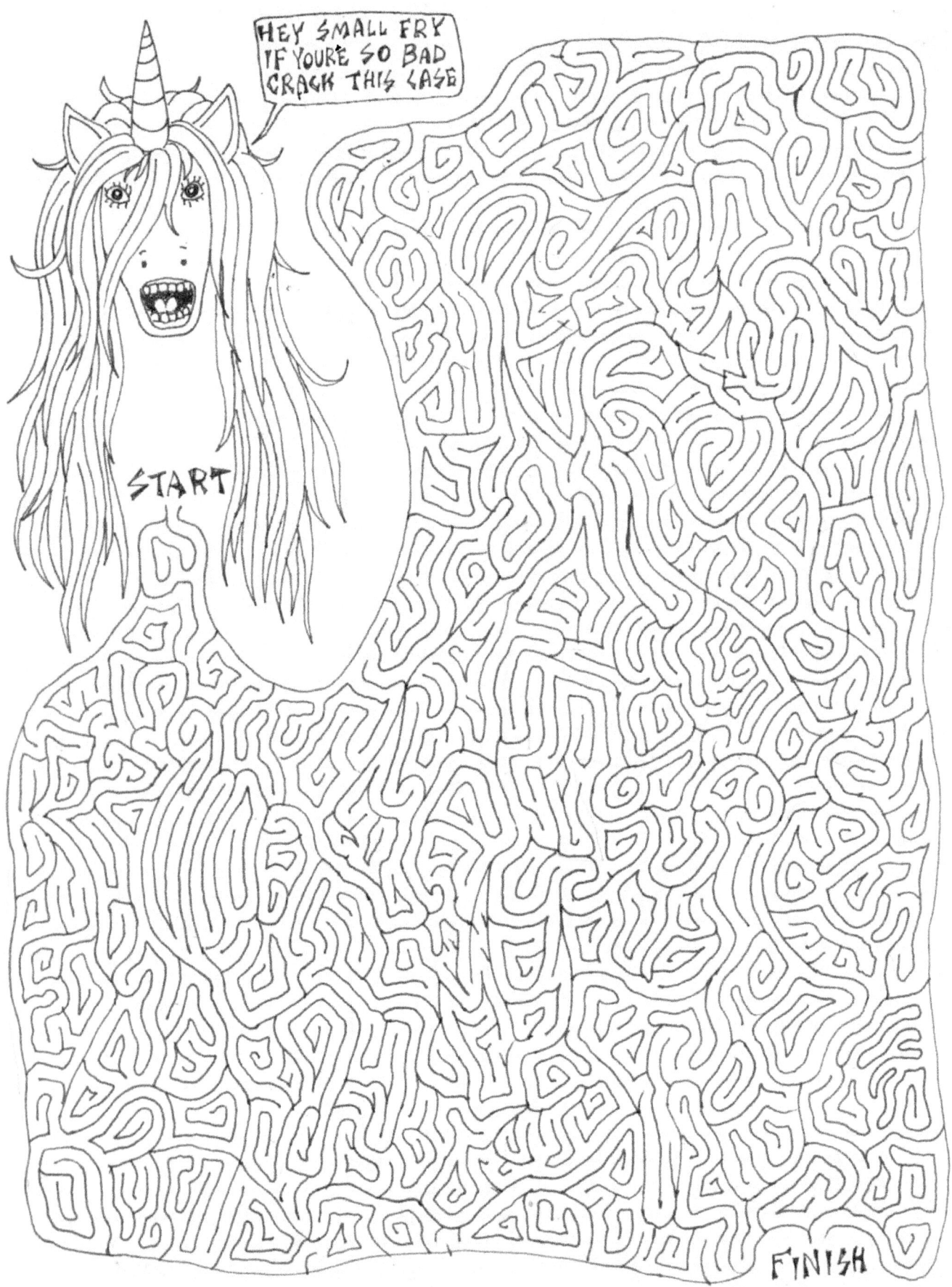

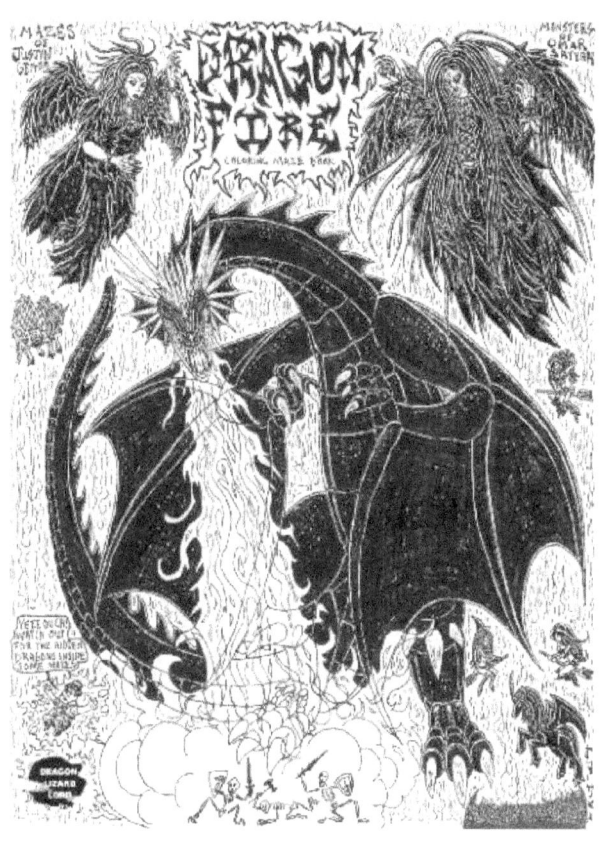

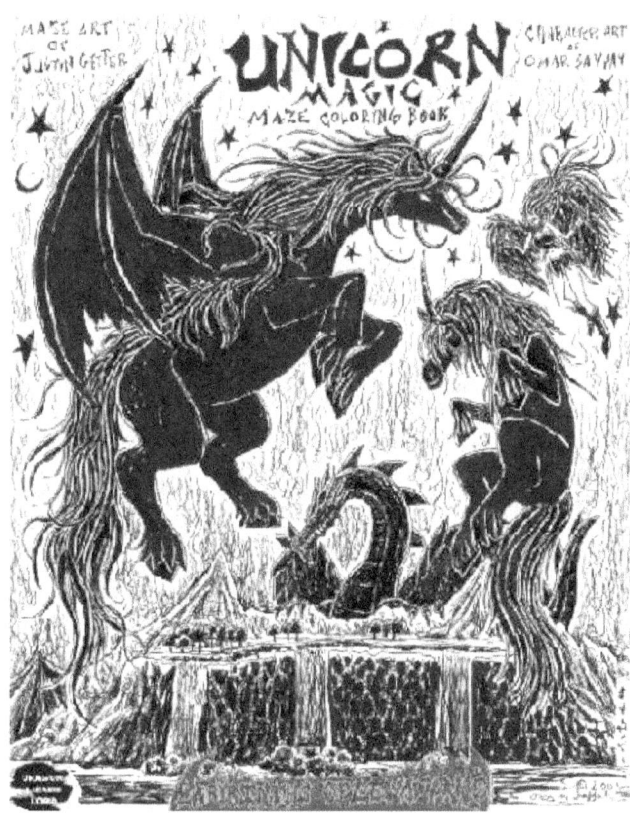

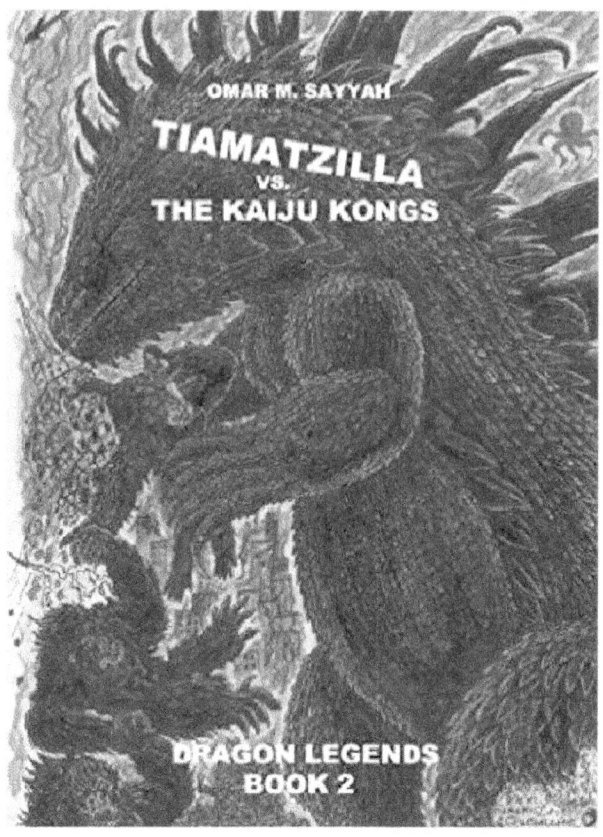

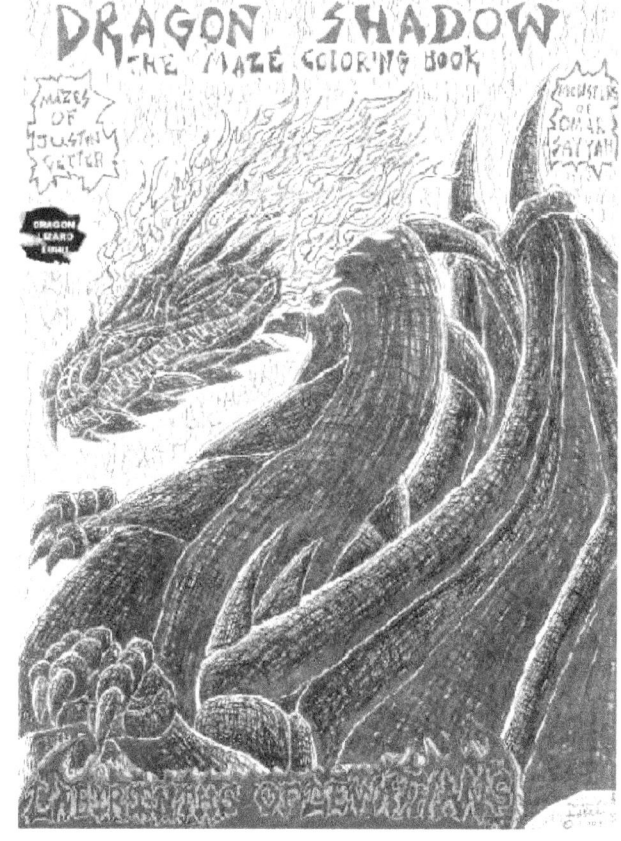

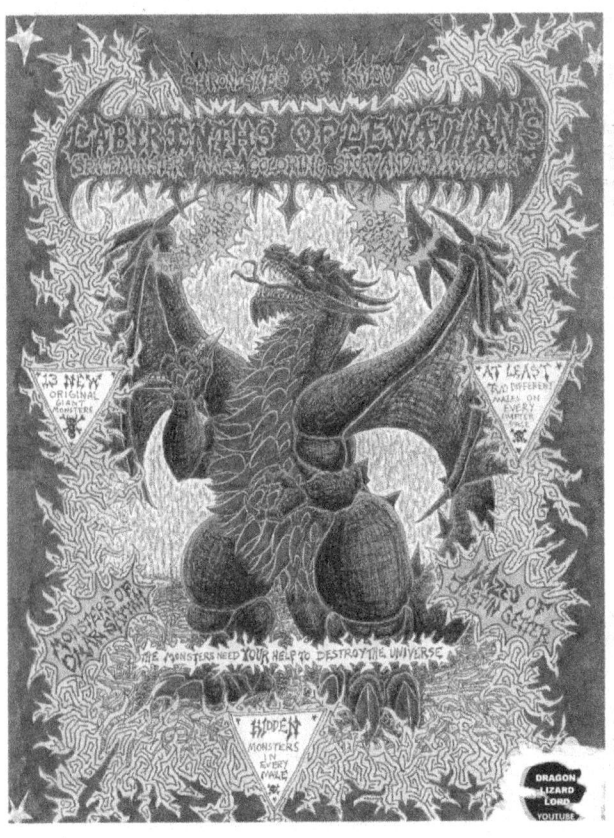

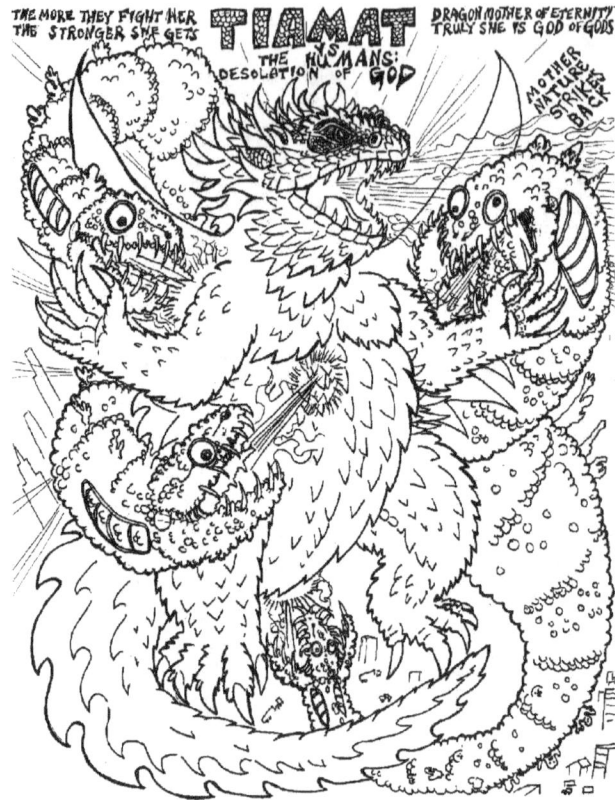

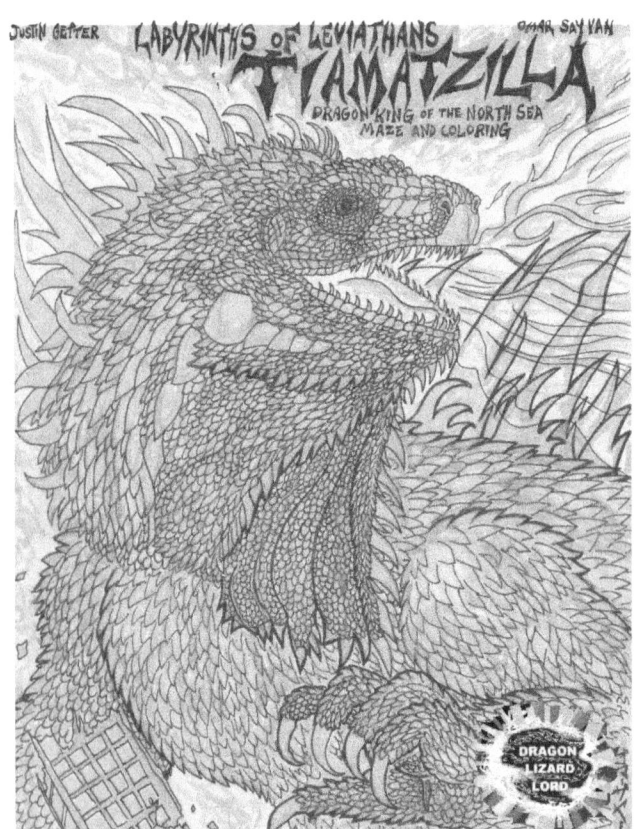

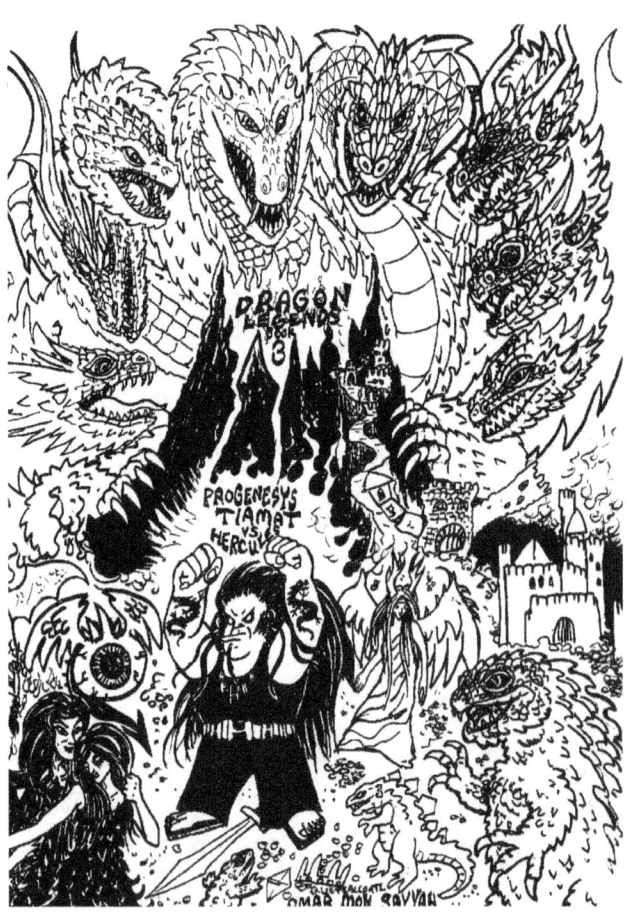